I0474690

Three Days atop A Mountain

On Sunday, March 5, 2017, we got stuck atop a mountain. Suffice it to say, we made it out alive else this little story could not have been written. But we were there for three days before help arrived. This is an original story coming from our own personal experiences. This is OUR story.

~Peggy

©Copyright 2019, Peggy A. Rowe-Snyder
No contents (writings, nor photos) not be reproduced for any reason unless there is prior written permission from the author. All photos were shot by and are the property of Peggy A Rowe-Snyder. High resolution copies of the photography can be obtained from the author. pegrowe@gmail.com

Dedication:

To my one and only true husband,

love of my life, Clyde L. Snyder.

My sister, Pamela & niece Desirae

and last and not least, my children,

Makkie, J. D., Wes, & especially, Diane Marie.

(#ShePersisted, #MeToo, #StillMyHero)

Without You, there would be no me...

joie de vivre

(The Joy of Living)

Illegitimi non carborundum

(Don't Let the Bastards Get You Down)

This all happened in a place called Tiller, Oregon the county of Douglas. At this particular time, I was a director on the board of the Douglas County Historical Society and my husband, was a medically retired ATM technician. We are both amateur photographers.

My husband is an antsy kind of guy. A man who must always be in motion in one form or another. That particular morning, he pointed out that we had summer season photos of South Umpqua Falls but we did not have winter season shots. So, after a little discussion we decided to do a day trip out to Umpqua National Forest and get those shots. The reader may wish to know that I did indeed bring up the fact that a storm was coming in and we might want to wait until another date. My husband pointed out that it was a short trip for us, we'd be home before the storm hit. It would get us out of the house, etc., etc.

We left our home in Tricity, also known as an area called the Missouri Flats in Oregon and headed first to Canyonville. We stopped at the local Burger King for breakfast. We saw our friend Sandra working that day. My husband teased her that she was stuck at work and we were going out to the Tiller area to take photos.

We enjoyed our normal chit chat with our friend and soon left on our little trip.

We headed out of Canyonville and toward Crater Lake on Tiller Trail Road (Douglas County Hwy. 1). We made it to Tiller and turned North on to South Umpqua Road, which turns into a National Forest Road (NF-28). Our destination was a total of nearly 29 miles from our home. We took photos all the way through.

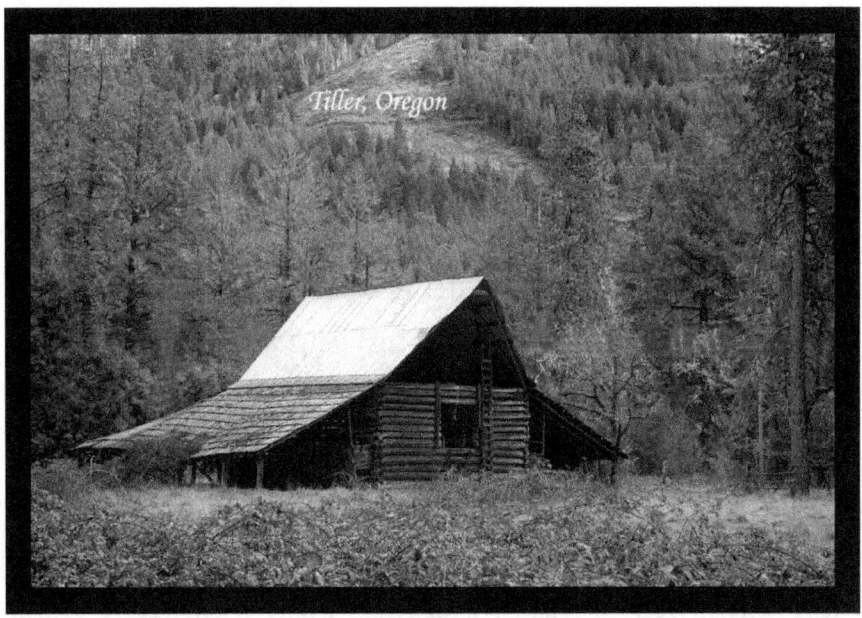

This old barn is up on South Umpqua Road outside of Tiller. My guess, due to its type of log construction and the stage of decay that it is quite old and probably ready for the list of National Historical Places.

Other than the beautiful sights we found, and the fact that we stopped to try and get a lot of good shots, our trip up was semi-uneventful. I say that because we did stop at one little way station on the way up. There were bathrooms there and needed a break. We each did our thing, took photos, and headed for the car. We soon found that we had locked ourselves out of the car (keys in the ignition) and my husband had to "break in" using a tree branch of all things. We got in the car, and he did his usual grumble and we both joked that perhaps we should just turn around and go home. One could take that experience to be a bad omen, though neither of us really believe in such a thing. So, we were joking more than anything else. But we were super happy that we were able to get into the car for the truth was that we were beyond cellphone range, and had no way to call for help from there.

South Umpqua Road follows the South Umpqua River through the South Umpqua National Forest. The South Umpqua is not the largest river in the world, but it's certainly not the smallest. In the winter when it is swollen it can be a wonderous sight, at least from a distance. The river bed is usually made of bedrock with sand bars, and boulders breaking up the scenery. An occasional log from a fallen Fir or Hemlock tree usually decorates the area and makes shelter for animals. In the Salmon breeding season these huge logs slow down the water flow and creates open areas out of the backed-up water. Salmon breed here in these areas.

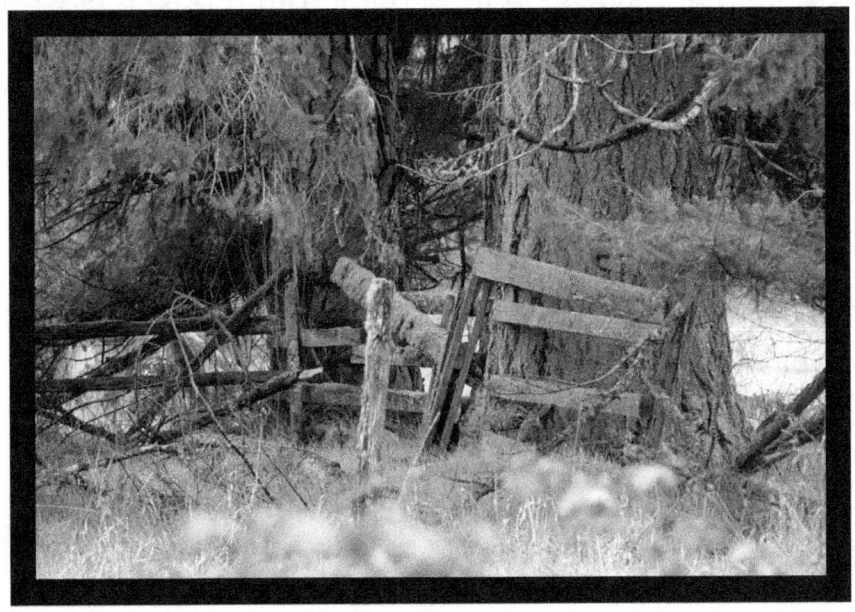

A view outside of Tiller, Oregon on South Umpqua Road.

We noted on the way up the road that there was snow above us. Just a dusting. We were driving an all-wheel drive Subaru Legacy. The car had proven its worthiness over and over again. It was a well-used car, and it showed. But it was also trusted. We stopped at a wayside for a bathroom break, a closed for the winter campground for photos, at some rock formations too. It was not meant to be a fast trip, it was meant to waste time and take the time to slow down, relax, enjoy each other's company, and talk. We got all of the above that day.

Photos on the next page: The same barn as in the shots earlier in the story. Outside of Tiller, Oregon on South Umpqua Road. Next page: Rock formations on South Umpqua Road, and again the same barn as in previous photos.

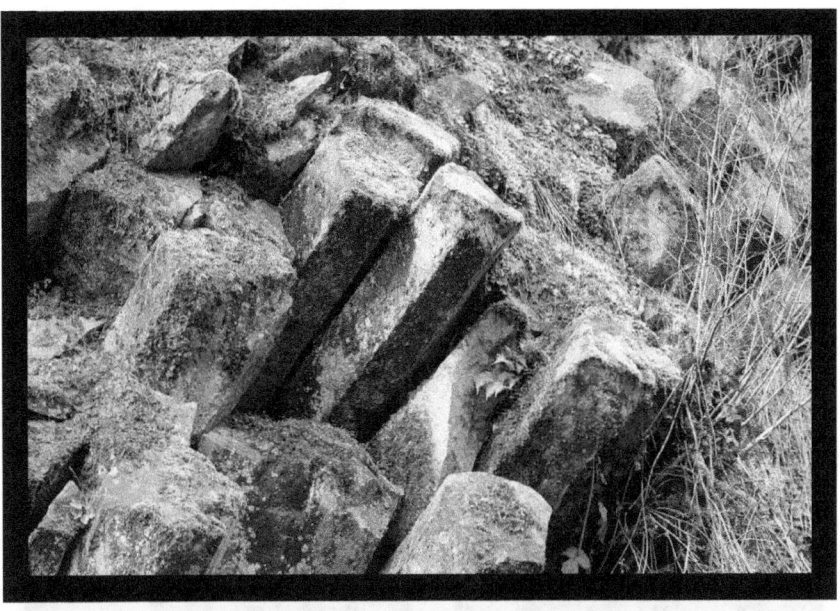

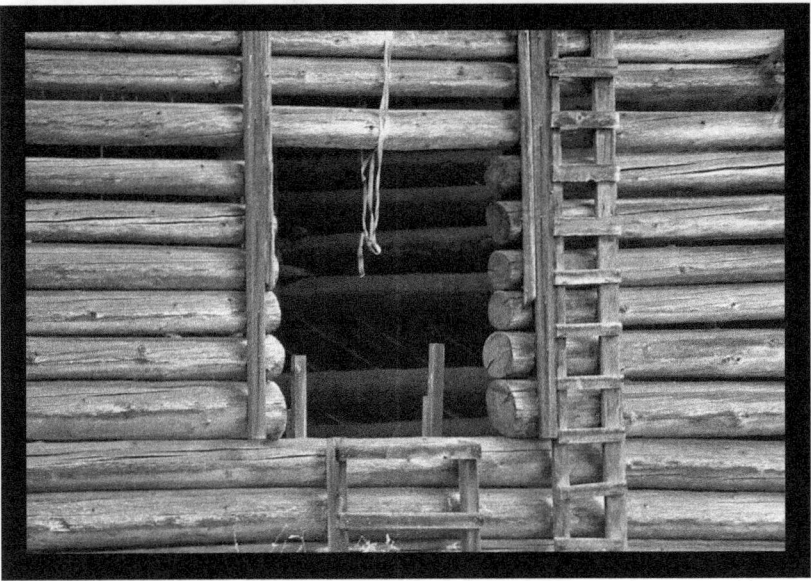

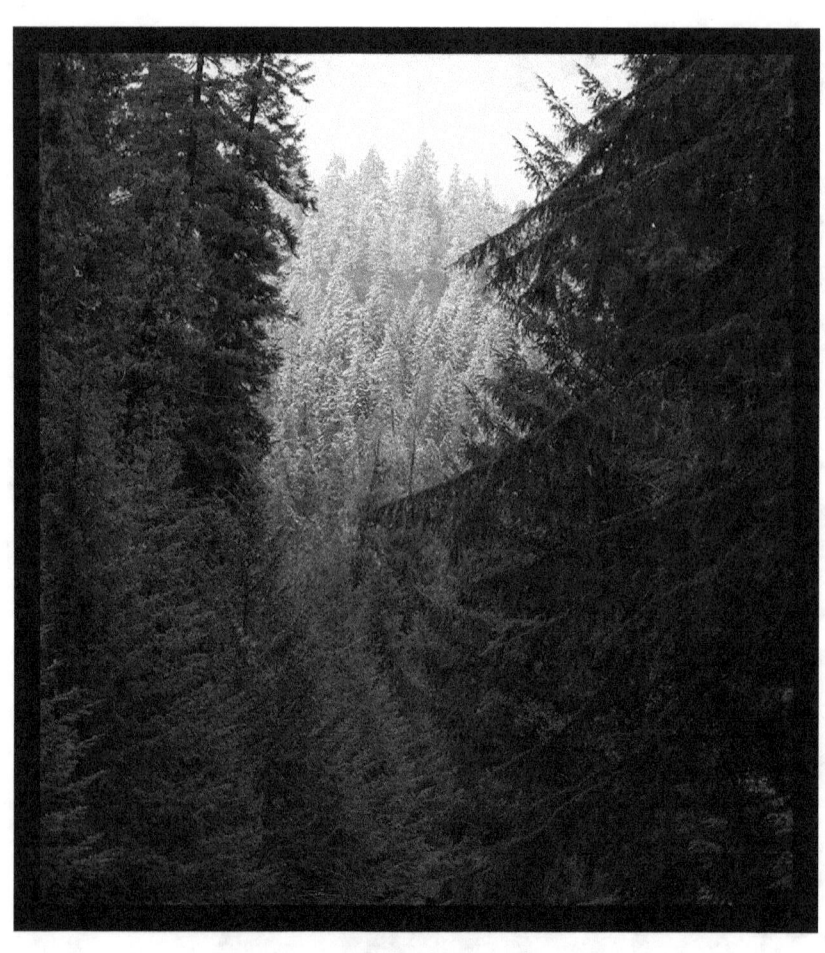

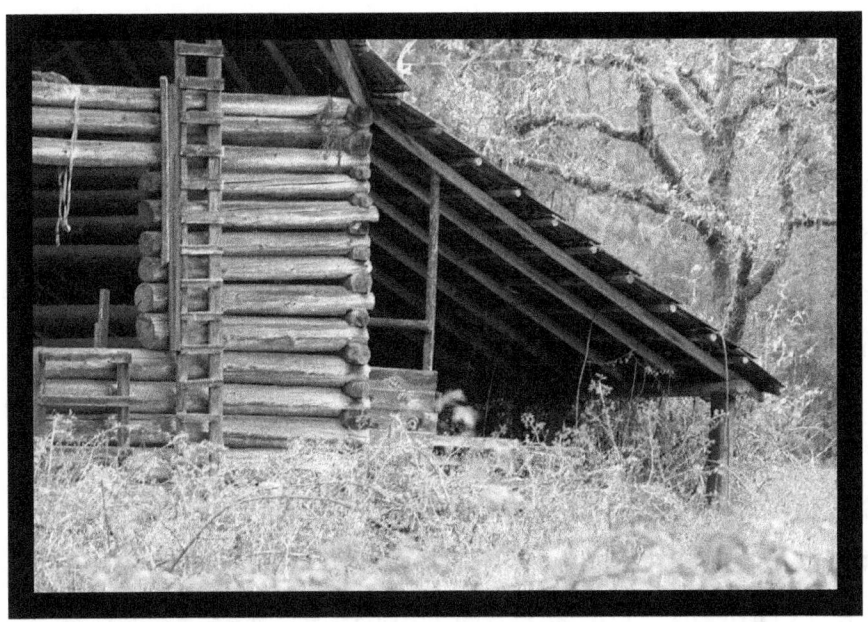

Photo from the previous page: Snow above the level of the road. If it had not been an overcast day, a really beautiful shot could have been had. Same barn, Tiller, Oregon.

After stopping several times for shots as we were rounding a mountain we actually ran into an inch or so of snow on the road and beyond. Buried beneath the snow on the road was one big and deep pot hole. A big and sharp stick also lay buried and unseen under the snow. Naturally, as per our luck, we hit the pothole and the stick and ended up with a flat tire.

You would think we would have gotten the message. Well, actually, one of us did. As my husband changed the tire and put a donut (temporary tire) the car he told me that we should turn around and go out the way we'd come in. The answer of course, was a resounding, "No". My logic and I said it was that we were now over half way over the road to Diamond Lake Boulevard, some 32 miles in. Roseburg lay on the other end, and so we were that much closer to a phone. There had been little to no snow to that point. We'd run into other drivers going the same direction as us and the opposite direction too. I wanted to go the fewest miles possible on that donut.

Well, right or wrong, I won that non-argument. Once the donut was on, we headed our way toward Diamond Lake Boulevard and Roseburg. The came up a discussion about how it was time to replace the tires, though that pothole was one of the biggest I ever saw.

Later after getting stuck, we actually discussed, not too seriously, suing the government for not properly maintaining the road.

More often we started seeing pockets of snow here and there, we were still running into drivers coming from the other way. The storm so far as we knew had not started yet. Though the sky was getting darker and darker. Other than a normal concern for being on a donut there was no other worries. There was no doubt in our minds that we were more than safe as we continued on our way.

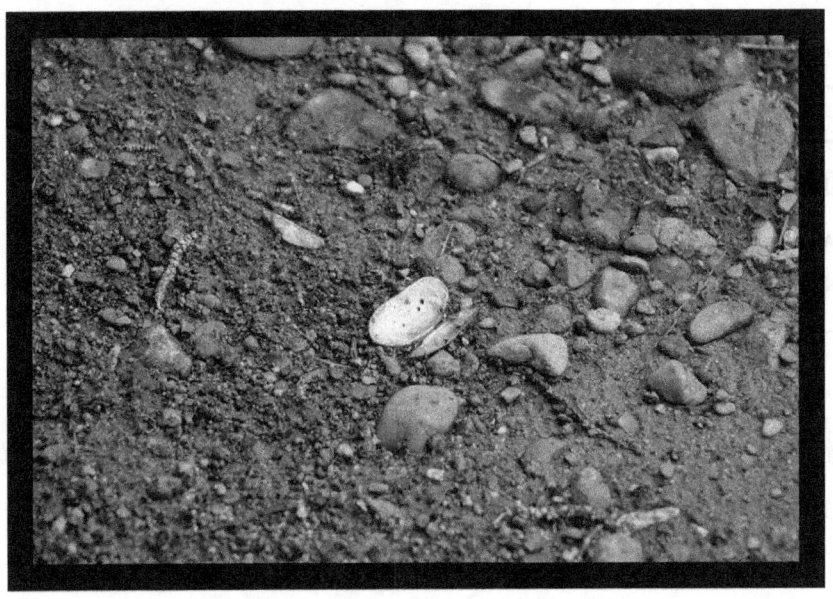

A mussel shell on a beach of the South Umpqua River.

We later found out from a National Parks worker that when we got stuck, we were on the North side of the mountain where it takes longer for snow to melt off. While I'm in this paragraph, let me just say when all this hit the media, news, et al, it was said we were lost. We were no where near lost. We had been on the road at least a couple times before and probably more than that. (I can't say how many times exactly), we were using a GPS system to back up our memory. We knew exactly where we were and we were NOT lost. We got stuck in the snow, not lost.

We rounded corner after corner, and drove past Dumont Creek Campground, took photos at Boulder Creek Campgrounds and of Campbell Falls. We drove past Coffeepot Creek, Ash Flat Campground along with Ash Creek.

Ash Flat Campground is in the Tiller Ranger Station District. It has a mix of hard and softwood trees all around it with a large wide open camp ground that is large enough to house several camp sites. We have seen the site full to it's maximum potential. We've seen it empty. It is my understanding that this is in the heart of the Umpqua Tribe of Cow Creek Indian heartland and if I recall properly, it is also where many a pow wow has been held by the tribe. My good friend

Clementine Rice just within the past few weeks passed away, and she is an elder of the tribe who organized the pow wow for nearly 20 years. If she were still with us, I'd give her a call and ask her for a short synopsis. Alas, she is not. I miss my good friend.

There is a fungus amongst us…

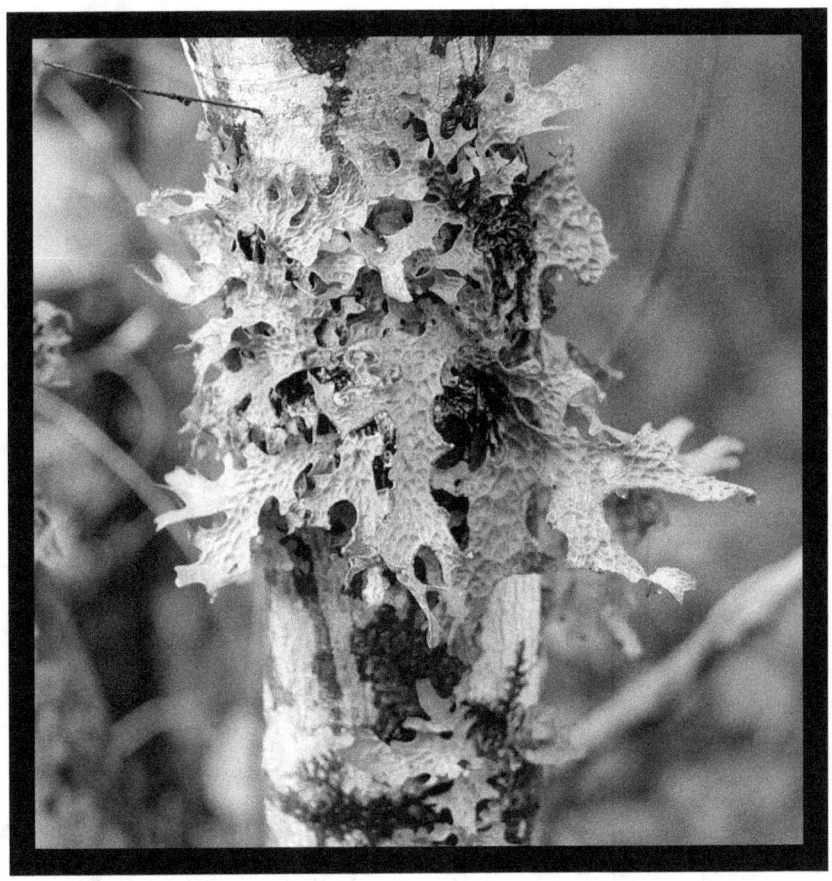

A noteworthy thing, if you have not already surmised it, the Umpqua Tribe of Cow Creek Indians are the native American's of this area. They were Douglas Counties first citizens. Though the county has a rich and interesting pioneer past to study, the Cow Creeks were here first, and it was they through very structured caring for the land cleared it with fire so that they had areas where they could hunt and live. So, my hats off to the survivors, all of them. The descendants who today, bear surnames of mostly French Catholic Church missionaries who came early in the pioneer season to teach and recruit the Cow Creek's to their faith and ended up taking up wives and creating families. These descendants today, make up the seven feathers, of the logo for the 7 Feathers Casino and their other business endeavors. Names include: Rondeau, VanNorman, Jackson, Dumont, Thomason, Crispen. This is, by no means, the full list, but you get the idea.

Although, this tribe was one of the first two tribes to have a treaty with the United States Government years ago, they survived never having a reservation as promised in the treaty. They stayed in their homeland for the most part. They survived the onslaught of the pioneers taking their land, and taking advantage of their kindness, and of disease, and more. The Cow Creeks have my deep respect.

We finally got to South Umpqua Falls, the object and subject of our trip into the mountains. We both got several (to say the least) shots. I've learned that you take way more photos than you need. That one good shot might be in there, might being the keyword. The great majority of my photos hit the bit bucket. He walked further downstream than I did. But he is also surer on his feet, and more practiced in the art of hiking. I am, in my 'old age' a tenderfoot, and allergic to pain. An inherited foot condition makes it painful to walk and stand. I usually don't go too far at all.

We got all the photos we wanted and felt satisfied with ourselves. We got back in the car and headed generally North, on the same National Forest road. We traveled up past Quartz Creek, Flood Creek, and Skillet Creek we traveled on. I watched the South Umpqua river disappear and reappear on our right. I noted more Fir and Hemlock trees as we climbed upward in elevation.

We reached Camp Comfort and stopped for a little stretch. We still had no clue what we were in for. The South Umpqua River turns into the Black Rock Fork (river or creek) around this area, and we mostly don't see it from the road. But I did notice we often could still hear its waters rushing by.

It was approximately 12 miles up the road from Camp Comfort very close to where the Black Rock Fork crosses the road and on the north side of a mountain that I still don't know the name of that we ran into a snow bank. The snow bank was only 4 to 6 inches deep, give or take. The depth was a height that the car had driven through before with success, more than once along our travels of the great Pacific Northwest. But we were on a donut, and to make a long story short, we high centered the car trying to get through it. We had a blanket, and we used it to try and get traction with. We used our Burger King cups to try and dig our way out. We tried several things, but nothing, not even the brute force of a leaded foot on the gas pedal could force the snow to give way of its hold. As we realized that we were tiring we also remembered that we'd just crossed paths with a young man in a pickup truck. We knew we were not the only people out there on the road. We sat down to relax in the car, and reasoned that someone would be along soon and we'd ask for help.

That Sunday afternoon sunset was at 6:08. Even though we were in a small clearing, and could hear the river rushing by we were surrounded by a lush and dark green forest of mostly Fir and Hemlock trees. The surroundings seem to make the night come on faster and fuller than normal. The dark was very, very dark. There were no street lights, no reflectors on the road, no tractor noises. There was not a porch light to be seen. All the things that we would normally take for granted and depend on for a sense of safety for the feeling of not being utterly alone were gone. We soon realized that for the night at least, we were alone, in our car, surrounded by an envelope of complete darkness, with not even shadows created by moonlight to give us heart. Our headlights were our lights, and we used them very rarely as they drained either gasoline or battery, both of which would be or could be lifesaving in our case. But, in order for me to break my sense of isolation the lights had to be turned on occasionally so that I could see that we were still, indeed, on planet Earth.

That first night was the absolute worst for me. Had we been out there for more than three days perhaps in the long run that would not have been the truth, but in the whole story for me the first night was the worst.   I grew up hearing about the Boogie Man, and how he crept about the night, waiting for children to leave their homes so they could be snatched up— for what, I have no clue.   I threated to run away once as a little girl, my father, again educated me about the Boogie Man. This little girl was too afraid to run away even though I was told to go ahead and pack my suitcase.

As the darkness fell completely, I worked myself into a silent tizzy. I was so shaken that my head trembled. I was scared beyond anything that I had known for a very long, long time. And that is if I had ever been that scared before. I was wanting to cry in a big, big way.   Time came and went when it was time to take our medications. We both have/had documented heart issues, sleep apnea that required a CPap, hypertension, and Diabetes, type 2. And that is only a partial list. I was very aware that all of those conditions could be fatal to us if left untreated for too long. Without medications my hypertension is quite severe, so I also knew that I had to work myself down and out of my fright, or else I'd kill myself via those conditions if I were not careful. At this point, I cuddled up to my husband and asked him if he were scared. He must have sensed my need of comfort and reassurance, or maybe it's just him and that's why I appreciate him so much for being rock solid, and dependable. His answer was that he had concerns, but at that point, he was not afraid. I made a mindful decision to lean on his confidence and find faith that it was going to be ok, and there was nothing to be afraid off. I felt the trembling cease, and my blood pressure come down. In my thoughts, I had to make up my mind that I was going to care for myself by doing the best I could to keep my body and mind under control. When I had the sense that I was about to lose control, I thought of my then 17-year-old daughter who was still at home and dependent on us and who was graduating that year. I also thought of my bi polar son, who will probably always need guidance in the future, and still did at that time. I thought of my older children who I hoped still wanted a cheer leader for a mother, and I thought of my grandson who probably didn't need me as much as I needed him... a joy in my life, a fantastic reason to get up each morning, the cuteness of that little brown head and mischievous smile. He was my pure delight.

We finally settled in for the night after coming to the conclusion that we were indeed, spending the night on the road and in our car. We began to make ourselves comfortable as we could. Yes, indeed, it was cold. In order to conserve our gas and make it last as long as possible we ran the engine, and the heater for about 20 minutes and sometimes less each hour. He had already unblocked the exhaust to make sure that none of that made it into the car. I awoke several times and I turned on our cell phones in hopes that they would ping a satellite, or accidently find a cell phone signal. We cuddled up together for warmth and comfort.

It was for sure a crude situation. There was no bathroom. I was and am to this day terribly scared of the dark. I still have nightlights on in my home. Believe me I am an expert in coming up with reasons why I need night lights so that I do not have to admit my fears. The stress caused an extreme loosening of the bowels. And though, we'd been married nearly 12 years, I was still too shy to allow anyone to be around while bodily functions were in process. I had to temporarily lay that shyness aside, hard as it was. What I discovered in the crudest sense is that people do what they need to do, period.

I woke up several times, and finally very faint shadows showed themselves. Most the time I could convince myself they were not the Boogie Man, but a tree. But the lights were turned on more than once so I could see there was no bear, no mountain lion or lynx. No Boogie men, no Big Foot, No Giant with his beanstalk. Sometime in the night, I woke up and saw snowflakes coming down at an alarming rate. At that moment in time they were beautiful and not. Snow had become a threat to survival, so there was no room for admiring the beautiful side in that moment. Besides I'd finally relaxed and was able to sleep as well as I could, and I wanted to sleep. I purposely woke myself several times during the night, listening for him to snore and trying to keep myself from snoring. Snoring or a snort, is a sign of the blockage of the breath of life. Sleep apnea raising its ugly head. I'd heard of it causing heart attacks. If I heard him, I gave him a light shake, enough to get him to adjust his body so that hopefully less of that went on. Luckily for us, we were forced into a semi-sitting position and it keeps the snoring and snorting mostly under control. I probably worried much more about it than I needed to. It was not a very restful night.

I awoke before he did. And my gosh, there was snow. Snow everywhere. Lots and lots of snow. Originally, when we got stuck, my husband had walked 100 feet or so either way and the snow was gone. We were in a lone snow bank. Now we were in a snow filled wonderland. The good side was we could see critter tracks if we needed to. The bad side was when we opened the car door, we had to push the snow out and away from the car to get anything done in the way of housekeeping. We determined that there was probably at least a foot of snow that hit the ground overnight. We were looking at a foot and half in total easily.

We realized in short order that morning, that we were going nowhere really, really fast. This is when we went into official survival mode. This is when any sort of conscious decision was made to survive. I am not sure that my husband ever had any doubt about our survival. Though he let me know he was sure he could reach humanity, I made him promise he would not leave me alone. At least, not until I was ready.

Hunger and thirst became an issue. We soon discovered that we could melt snow in front of the heater outlet in the car, and there we had water. For food, well, that was another story. I knew that we needed to eat something to keep our sugars at least stable. With a type 2, Diabetic having sugars too low or too high was very dangerous, or could be. The only thing we had in the way of food in the car was left over dog food from a trip we'd made to Fort Bragg

(Mendocino County, California) to visit my husband's mother. Well, there was that and a few packets of honey mustard sauce, and also some packets of ketchup.   I encouraged my husband to eat, partake of the dog food, which was a dry kibble from Costco (Kirkland brand even!). We did not have to like it or love it. We did not have to be full. We had to keep our sugars level, and stave off the hunger. He declined at first, eventually eating very little. Later in the day, I tried the ketchup and mustard – dog food really is yukky. If we all tasted what our dogs ate, we'd probably not feed it to our animals. The texture is rough, sandy even. Ketchup helped, honey mustard did not.   But I joked that we now had gourmet fare, and tried to prod my husband to eat. Over the long haul, I think he ate once, a few bites probably to please me, without the gourmet toppings.

As the second day progressed it became obvious that we would not see one body that day. It had snowed enough to either block traffic, or people just were not testing the environment yet. Yet, we hoped some 4x4 group, or folks with ATV's would wander by. It was sometime in that early morning of the 2nd day (or first day depending on how you count them) that my 17-year-old daughter called 911. She woke up and realized that we'd not made it home yet. I could not tell you in what order everything happened in from that end. But I can tell you over the long haul, the kids were told that our chances of coming out alive with our health issues was slim to none. I am thankful beyond measure for the folks who checked in with my daughter to comfort her, and get her what she needed, help her with the heater, etc. She was one tough cookie, she called family, kept everyone appraised, released news via Facebook, and coordinated with authorities the best she was able. When all was said and done, after hearing from my sister what a trooper my child was, how brave she was. After getting home, I told her how proud I was of her, and how I knew I never had to worry about her, she was going to be ok. I had at least one survivor on my hands, and in this case, it was a very good thing.

But we were not home yet. During the 2nd night a repeat of the 2nd. Except it felt much colder to me. I'd been outside of the car in the snow just enough that my snow boots were wet, and my feet could not get warm even in the boots. We'd already moved to the backseat in order to be more comfortable. We tried the very back, putting down the back seats, but it just didn't work. We were too big, or the space too small, we could not sit up, it just didn't work.

In order to survive the cold, and in effort to conserve our gasoline and make it last as long as possible, we made a doggie 'hammock' (a seat cover to keep the dog hair off the car seat) into a blanket, and covered our heads with it. We huddled and cuddled. He carefully cut the front car seat covers off the seats. With one he fashioned a sort of blanket to be used as another layer. We took turns using it.   The other seat cover became a sack. He lined it with the extra fabric for insulation, he had me put my feet in and then he put his feet in with mine. His feet finally warmed mine. It was a romantic and kind thing to do. It caused me to love and respect him all the more.

Today, this three-day experience has come to be called as our 'Winter Retreat'.   It is we, my husband and I, call it our 'Winter Retreat' because for us though, there was a ton of stress for everyone else involved for us it was a retreat. It was a break from family issues, bi polar disease and its drama, a 17-year-old who did not want to listen or even participate (ahem, drama). A break from financial hardship, the realities of aging and ill health, the struggle with depression, the fact that we are both survivors (of childhood sexual abuse & domestic violence) and live with the consequences of that. I had the strain from the caring about a dying non-profit and the wonderings and thoughts I had about how to go about saving the organization. That issue hung over me like a lead weight.

There was the heartbreak of divorce, ours. I filed for divorce after more than ten years of a happy marriage, not because I was unhappy in anyway. But, because we could not afford health insurance for me, not even with help from the ACA health law. With heart issues one does not go without insurance. Medicine with its modern wonder devices and pills are what have kept me alive more than once. For example, I've sported a dual chamber pacemaker since 2004. I brag that I have a 'dually.' A divorce was nothing either of us wanted, but I filed and he did not contest. There was nothing much to fight over. The house was always in his name, his Jeep was his before we met. My car was mine. He promised that he'd pay me back the money I'd put down on the house. There was no anger, no blame, no bad behaviors, no frustrations between us (other than the normal ones you get in life). It was all over health insurance and staying alive. We were both hurt beyond measure. Tears were the order of the day, each of us, in our own time. Frustration, anger, hurt.

Depression, and not thinking that the hurt was ever going to come to an end. It was when I learned that marriage was NOT just a piece of paper, and that the piece of paper was really, really important to us both. Marriage is a partnership, and what I learned was that it was a partnership between ourselves and our maker. And a piece of paper or lack thereof, did not make or break that partnership. It is 2019, we still live together, laugh together, get mad at each other, disagree over the kids together, love together, legally out of marriage, but spiritually and in our heart of hearts, very much married.

My husband and I have never had a real communication problem. The worst of it is when either of us hesitates to speak for fear of hurting the other. I was helped a lot in women's (Seeking Safety) group when I heard the words, "It's not what you say, it's how you say it." On that mountain, we talked about everything. Came to new conclusions, found some new dreams, rescued some foundering emotion, became again one another's best friends. We recommitted, in our way, to our future together. Even if we had passed on to the great beyond, there is no way, we'd left that space unhappy or ungrateful for what had become of us. As a married couple, we found more depth and breadth than we'd ever found before. We came out stronger and together better than ever. That time on the mountain helped keep us afloat and it saved our relationship. Maybe it was our 'marriage retreat.'

I woke in the 2nd night, to see yet more snow falling. Big beautiful flakes. This time I knew it met that we were in even more danger than I was before. It finally hit my consciousness that we were now in grave danger, and that there was a good chance that we were going to die unless something gave. I spent sometime wondering how one can see such beauty falling around oneself, and yet have such terrible thoughts about survival. But this was the reality – we needed to be worried. And the snow was very pretty.

I woke before him, but we both woke pretty early that next day. Day three in my mind. After two nights in the middle of nowhere and on top of a mountain, and into our third day of being stuck on top of the same mountain, I began the day by again realizing and then voicing that we had a good chance of dying up there. My husband had already offered to walk to get help.

I had issues with him trying to go and get help. The man had open heart surgery one year into our marriage. It had long since healed, but buried deep in my psyche in terms of partnership and being a helpful partner in life. I saw a long walk as a threat to him specifically. And then there was the fear of being truly alone. What if I met a bear while all alone? Could one break into the car, what would I do? He was carrying a Derringer; he was licensed to do so. But the Derringer would do no good against a bear or mountain lion. And it wasn't going to do me any good with it in his pocket. I'm sure that some of my fears were rational and others were not. Either way I had to determine that I would live through it, survive…and then I had to decide to let him go.

I'm sure I became somewhat of a whiner. If I was going to die out there, I wanted it to go a certain way. I wanted to be found in a certain way. I wanted to write my kids messages…. I started to voice my fears. Somewhere in the in-betweens, during the silences, my husband asked, "Are you ready for me to save your life yet?". Words I will never forget. It almost sounded fun. He sounded full of certainty. If there was fear, he did not show it. He's always had this very quiet self-confidence. I really had to think about this. This was truly a huge decision. In some ways it was a debate, was I going to die alone, or with him? How do you put aside such a primal fear?

Again, I leaned into his confidence, which is something I've always done with him on a very regular basis. I finally answered in the affirmative. "Yes, you may save my life. Yes, you can leave me alone, no, I don't want to do it, no I don't want you to go, but I know you have to go, it's the only chance we have."

It seemed that things went into fast forward. He was anxious to leave which at first puzzled me. Later I remembered that time was indeed, of the essence and there was a method behind what I considered madness. Once again, it was survival, pure and simple.

I went into a mode just like the one I go into when I was getting him ready for work. Making his lunch in a sort of way, and dreaming up ways to try and make things easier for him. He had one hell of a job before him. For his 'lunch' I bagged him some dogfood and I told him to eat a little something no matter how awful it was. I implored him to keep his strength up, and his sugars constant. I am positive that I probably reminded him (yet again, broken record, Peggy) about the horrible side effects of high sugars. I made him a 'rainhat' from a little black plastic grocery bag provided by our local convenience store (thank you, Nick & Saherra Sharma). I dug out paper clips (giant ones) and my note book and I made "help us" notes on paper and on paper plates (left over from our trip to Fort Bragg.) I wanted plastic bags to put over his shoes…. I wanted him bundled up and warm. I wanted him to go and get it done, and I did not want him to go all at once. Oh!! To be human!

The man, MY HERO, walked very close to 12 miles to get me off the top of that mountain. Along the way, he was pretty sure he had an encounter with a Mountain Lion. He definitely encountered a lot of snow. He made it to one residence but no one was home. Finally, he ran into a National Forest Road Crew. They had to think he was a nut wearing a black plastic bag hat. After a little discussion the two young men realized they had run into the 'missing' man of the couple. They called dispatch for help. Dispatch told them to have my husband call a tow truck. Dispatch didn't get it. The two young men were denied permission to help, but they did it anyway.

They drove their truck as far as they could up the mountain and then one of them, who I am sure was an angel in disguise, hiked up to check on me. He introduced himself to me, checked my gasoline levels, determined that I'd be ok while folks got their ducks in a row to help me. He promised me they'd be back.

Gave me a time line, and promised me again. I'm not sure I've ever said thank you to God so many times.

Once my husband left for his very long walk sometime probably between 9 and 10 am, I wasn't sure just what to do with myself. I wrote a note to one of the kids. I tried to write poetry (one of my old standby's in terms of getting by emotionally). I did some thinking. But, mostly, I did some sleeping. I wrapped myself up in our doggie blanket, and put my feet back in the car seat sack, I used the other car seat to make a sort of pillow since I didn't have a chest to lean into. I woke and I ate a piece or two of dog food and I hoped that he was doing the same.

After about four hours, I woke up from one of my naps. It was still daylight, though probably afternoon. I was looking around and realized that there was a drawing or perhaps artwork on the driver side window. On closer inspection, I realized that it looked like someone drew a kind of double cross in the condensation. Now, my rational mind thought, that the downward stroke on the cross was quite easily explained. The condensation broke into water form, and it dripped down taking the little tiny bits of water down the glass with it. What confused me what the two cross lines... condensation runs down and not across. It is movement that is fed by gravitation.

Let me inject here that to believe in God has been somewhat of a fight for me. I was raised by an atheist mother who had no problem sharing her belief in a very strong way. When I asked and got an answer from her, I was left, as a child, speechless by her strength of disbelief. Of course, when your mother says it, it must be true. A one-time statement has stuck my entire life.

My father on the other hand, while not practicing was raised a 7th Day Adventist by a non-believer mother, and a 7th Day Adventist father. My father fostered some belief. One of the most beautiful things he ever said to me was that he believed we were like butterflies. When a human on earth dies, it enters a new phase of life. It breaks free from its cocoon and enters another form and it lives another life. He believed and believed we should go to church but he did not believe quite enough to take us to church.

So, I grew up with parents at almost polar opposites in terms of religion. A child can feel these things, even when words are not spoken, the child knows. It has had its effect.

I have spent some time in churches. I was baptized into a Southern Baptist Church. I was totally sincere at the time. But I began to question things. And I foundered again into disbelief. It did not help that my husband at the time, while preaching hellfire and brimstone cussed and said the F-word every other word out of mouth, and destroying my property, using drugs, lying, etc. etc. etc. I could not at that time, accept the humanity of the situation. How does live a life where they cannot practice what they preach?

I church shopped on and off for a while and found myself eventually at Geyserville Christian Church in Sonoma County, California. This little church on highway 101, is still my church home. It is where I found my ultimate idea of what faith and belief is, what and who God really is. What love and faith means? A shout out with a big hug for Pastor Hilary F. Marckx.

And so, the very short fight in my mind as I looked at the double cross on the driver side window came to a close. There was no gravity that could pull water sideways, and even though it looked like a kid made the cross with finger art, or perhaps a dog had used his nose to draw the image, the truth is, that I took it as a message. I took it as something positive.

I realized that I could see through the cross, and it seems obvious but the optics were part of the message. The world and the universe are a mighty big place. Beyond the cross was a small baby evergreen tree, topped with snow and bent over by the weight. But it was still green, and one could see it was a survivor. Come spring that tree was going to stand back up straight and carry on. The double cross looked to me like two people who were arm in arm. One stood just slightly above the other. The general message of the cross itself was that I was being carried or assisted along. I was not alone. When I felt weak someone was there to help me up and onward. Ultimately the message was one of survivorship – once again, all would be well. No matter how I felt in life, I was never, EVER alone. And I wrapped myself up in that message, and spent the rest of my time with the faith of knowing all would be ok even if I had a few more tough times ahead.

I will be ending this story quite soon, as the story really does end quite soon. Suffice it to say that two young men, basically got up to the top of the mountain with what looked like a golf cart or a hunting cart. It held two people so one had to ride outside on the back once I was loaded in.

There were times when the vehicle could not make it over a hump and these heroic young men got out and actually pulled the vehicle, and myself up and over with their bodies, just like a horse might be used to pull a trailer. They also used a winch. I discovered on this ride that the National Forest Service sometimes uses special safety straps when winching from a tree, in effort to not damage the trees in the forest. I appreciated that.

The Snowcat that belonged to Douglas County was out on another mission. So, a Snowcat from Josephine County was called in. It arrived about the time that I was officially out and with others. I saw it parked, and still trailered on my way out, I think, somewhere around Camp Comfort. I would have been fun to get to ride in it. But I think what ended up happening is far more spectacular.

How many times in one life time do you hear of people literally towing another person to safety with their bodies as if they were pack animals? What kind of person does it take to do this? What motivates them? In my mind the answer is quite touching. I asked a professional people person about these questions. The answer was that these people love helping people, and getting someone out alive and well is the big payoff for them. Can you imagine caring for your neighbor that much?

The two young men, angels in disguise, got me to, I think Camp Comfort, and transferred me to a pick up with a young man. This is where I found out that my husband was ok, and that he was waiting for me up the road.

I want you to know that along the way down from the mountain I saw teams of people staged every so often. There were men and women. I even recognized a few faces (my daughter went to a nearby school, Days Creek school) –I recognized a few names. I saw loggers standing by a fire. Most of the time folks were waving us on down. Until it happens to you, you really have no idea what kind of team work is involved in getting one (or more) persons to safety once they've been lost.

Next I was transferred to an ambulance and its crew, who took my vitals and asked me a couple of key questions. When they asked me, who was President I really had to think it through. And I don't believe in having the horrible attitude that I have towards the man in the White House, but I still don't like him, and I still don't claim him as my President. I see him as a predator, and I'll never see anything else.

I was deemed healthy, as my vitals were good. I was released to go home. My husband's vitals were already checked and acceptable.

We entered a pickup driven by Jerry. A very nice man who drove us home. It was a long and fun ride. It was really dark so it was hard to see where we were going, and I think that is what it made such a long ride for me. Somewhere along the line Jerry stopped and we were offered a cookie or breakfast bar or something. It was really good. At another short stop a lady offered me coffee. I am not a coffee drinker, but I must tell you that was the best coffee I'd ever had in my life. It was probably the best I'll ever have in my life. I have spent all my adult life trying not to take anything for granted. After this experience, I couldn't even take the taste of coffee for granted.

It was around 10 pm when we got home. We walked around to the back door, which in reality we installed and used as a front door. As the door opened, I saw the face of my 17-year-old daughter. It was extremely tear streaked. She had been crying and crying and crying. I was filled with empathy and pride all at the same time. We called my mother in law, and my sister, and then took our medications, took a much-needed shower, and settled down to sleep.

The next morning, I faced Facebook, which turned out to be ok. And we heard the realities that existed when we were gone on our 'Mountain Retreat'. My son started looking for someone to make house payments so he'd have a place to live. My youngest was obviously worried about having a place to live to finish school. My oldest informed them that she'd take control of the property because she was the oldest and the first heir, and they would be paying her rent. When it was pointed out to her that was not what mom and dad wanted, she pointed out that courts often overturned what people said they wanted in their documents. The attitude that I heard from my two youngest left me with a really bad taste in my mouth. I did not see a sibling trying to help two younger ones. I saw someone trying to position themselves to be in control and power to do with property anything they pleased.

My second oldest showed up with her husband while we were gone, and helped her with the heat. Apparently, she kept most of her opinions to herself. Not all, but most. Neither she nor my oldest called to see if one or both of us were ok. That was unexpected and it hurt beyond words.

My son, who is bi polar and on the autistic spectrum, and also has a pretty bad case of PTSD was in turn victimized while we were gone by a family 'friend'. Someone his age, that actually spent a lot of time with us when he was a boy. We trusted him. My son handed him the keys to my husband's Jeep, and asked him to drive around to find us. Which they did. But there were four people in the Jeep, so I am unsure just where they would have put us had they found us. At some point, the 'friend' decided to see if the Jeep could do what it was built to do. Drove it into a muddle puddle that had he been an okay driver he could have easily maneuvered out of. But he floored it and slammed it from drive to reverse. He tore out the rear end (including the spider gears), trashed the transmission and then didn't have the guts to tell us once we were home. They brought it home, parked it and hoped that Clyde would not notice that his license plates were bent, that the inside had been flooded, and that it the machine could not switch gears. We paid nearly $2,000 to fix the rear end, only to find out that the transmission was destroyed too. We found out later, as the smaller details came out that this 'friend' and his girlfriend had repeatedly told my son to get used to the idea that were dead and to get on with life.

This friend wanted our son to open my husband's gun safe. Luckily the kids have no clue where the combination is to this day.

The 'friend' and his wife, were down and out, and we offered them the use of our old RV and tentatively sold it to them. No money ever changed hands, the title was not signed over, and as the truth slowly came out over the period of several days, they were eventually asked to leave. We've seen him once, and he acted like nothing was wrong. My son has seen her once, and she acted the same. It is hard to believe that someone we trusted was so willing to take advantage of ourselves and our kids.

As for my oldest, I told her that before she starts planning, next time, make sure we are DEAD FIRST. Because her assumptions were all wrong. She has a case of MS, and we had already decided that she was not going to be the person to handle our estate(s) – as it would add more stress to her life. We'd made other arrangements. At this point it is our two youngest that we worry about the most, although, the truth is, they've both shown themselves to be survivors, and I am proud of that. They'll be ok no matter what.

As I come away from this experience, I am able to think better of most human beings and my belief in the basic goodness in humans was justified. I saw so many good people coming off that mountain. I could bake thank you cookies for the rest of my life, and never, ever feel as if I'd repaid a debt.

My faith in God, or our Higher Power, The Word, Jesus, or any other name that you wish to call the Love that holds our universe and lives together has been strengthened. I live in a mostly quiet testimony to the power of the great Father or Mother, or whatever it is. I will not presume to know.

We had churches praying for us up and down the west coast and as far East as Wisconsin (that I am aware of). I've always believed in the power of prayer and/or positive thought. I read Jung as a young woman, and it impressed me. I thank each and every person who thought about us, and send up their prayers in our behalf. I saw this power in action. I saw God plant people around us who could help us. I saw Him give my husband, who had a heart blockage, and a bad aortic valve walk 12 miles to get home. For that matter, I thank the U. S. Army for giving him lifesaving survival skills. Most of all, I am thankful for the lesson in humility, and a relearned gratitude for all around me... even if it's a rock on the ground, or a child who is really getting on my nerves.

What I know, beyond a shadow of a doubt is that in those days, I was blessed in a big, big way. I still am. I always will be.

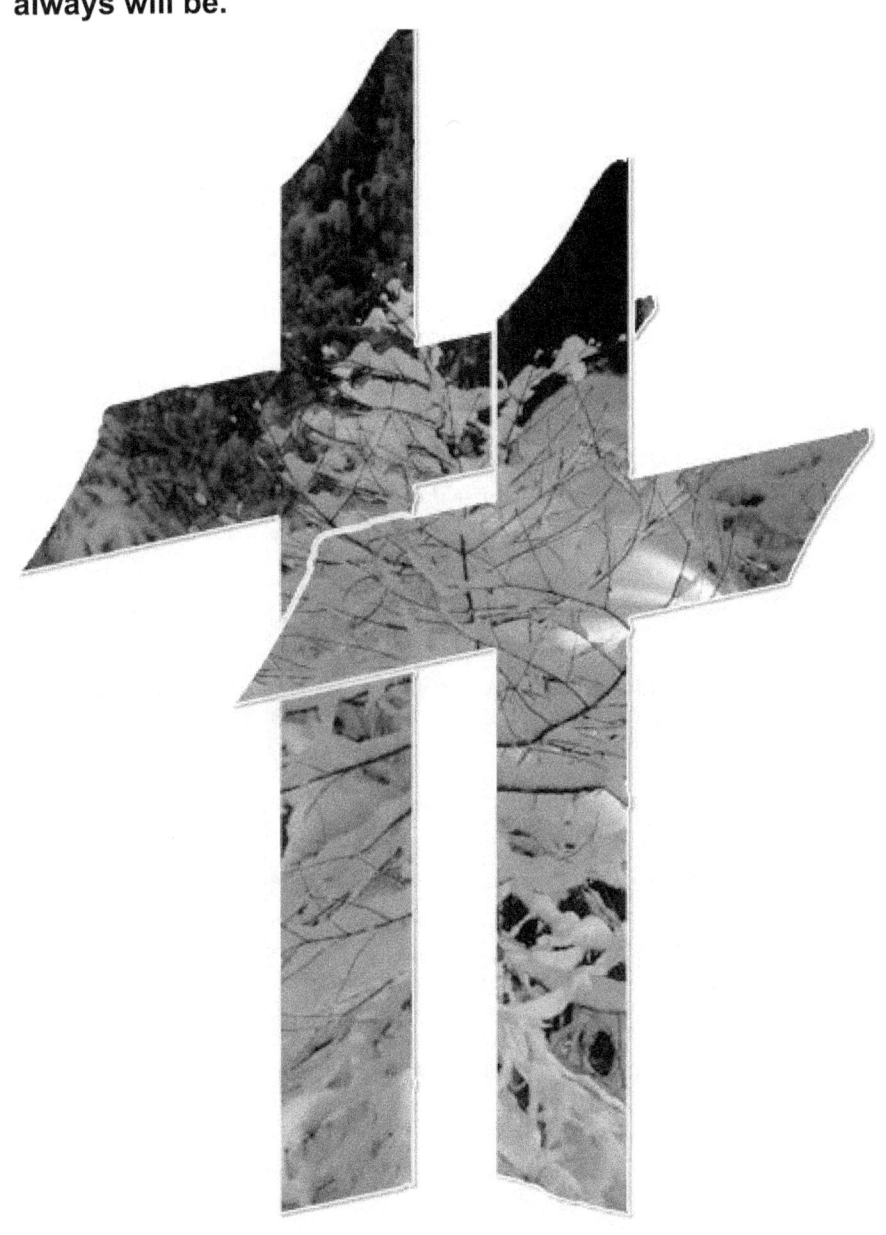

Graphic above: Two Crosses, by Peggy A. Rowe-Snyder

From my Facebook page, posted March 8, 2017: These crosses are pretty similar to the what I saw on the driver side window of the car, about 15 minutes before the first crew showed up to let me know that help was on the way.

I put a photo in the background to help keep in mind what the frame of mind that I was in-- what was in the background.

The Christian reference is obvious. But I had realized that this was the second set of crosses that I had seen in two days. The message was pretty obvious. God wanted me to remember that he was there, and holding us in his arms.

But I also saw the two crosses---and realized how well they symbolized two people, with their arms intertwined. And, it was easy to see myself and Clyde. Partners, intertwined, locked together, acceptable toward ourselves, God, and all others.

A lot of realizations hit me in those moments-- I realized how lucky and loved that I truly am. That I am really luckier than most. There came sense of peace and resolution that I have waited for, literally for years. I had to let things go, and accept everything just the way it is. My hang ups were my problem, and I did not need them anymore.

Happily, I'm pretty sure that I can go into my PTSD group for women and tell them that I did my homework (rethinking things in a positive light)

What being stuck in the snow does for one's sense of humor…

Posted on March 17, 2017

(note: there are times when a sense of humor just carries us through a hard time. You laugh, else you cry. In this case it was that and more, a healthy release from a hard time. It is two years later, and obvious to me, is my ability to romanticize the past. This is a window in to the situation, despite the humor, only a few days after getting home from the mountain.)

Thursday, March 16, 2017

To Whom It May Concern,

My husband and I had the bad luck of having to stay in our car and 'survive' in the snow atop a mountain this week. This 'survival' mode only lasted for two and a half days.

We arrived Sunday afternoon to only around 2-3 inches of snow after changing our flat tire. Our low riding 4×4 Subaru Outback Legacy ™ got caught on a very small snow drift. We used our poor dog's blanket to try and get traction and get out, but alas our Subaru ™ was unable to use the Bratz ™ blanket.

We were unable to even dig our car out using simple Snapple bottles ™ where the bottom had been cut off in order to dig our way out. I promise, I kid you not!!!

We decided to make ourselves comfortable and stay the first night. We'd passed trucks coming from the other direction, we were sure we were safe. Soon, the snow began to fall! It just went on and on and on. It continued to fall even more. The next morning, we were probably buried in a foot of snow. At this point, we became acutely aware that we were probably in trouble.

I remembered that we had told our friend, a manager at Burger King ™ in the nearby town of Canyonville, Oregon that we were going to take photos at South Umpqua Falls and so I wasn't much worried at all. Well, at least for a while. I was glad that I had even made sure to pack the extra ketchup packet from our food and stash it away in my pocket. Burger King ™ uses Heinz™ brand you know!!

Well, that next day under a foot of snow. We had to figure out how to survive. It's sad but it's true, that I learned the hard way that Eberhard's ™ Ice Cream buckets are not only good for storing away dry dog food for long trips, but they also make very good toilets! I have to admit that Kirkland paper towels make excellent toilet paper in a pinch.

We were soon thirsty and realized we'd be drinking melted snow. So, we cut the bottoms out of an Aquafina ™ water bottle. The bottle became a very good snow scooper for letting the snow melt in (leave the lid on, turn upside down and it will stand in your drink stand), hence providing refreshing **and life giving (no name brand, generic)** water.

After our first night in the forest, I have to admit that my stomach began to feel a little pained. I started to be concerned about what we would eat. I knew my husband had a small, two shot American Arms™ 410/45 Long Colt Derringer on his body, and so I prayed for a bunny to hop by. Then I remembered we had no way to start a fire, and so, I realized that more than likely lunch would be the Kirkland ™ Lamb & Rice dog food so highly recommended by our dogs' vets over at DCLVS in Roseburg, Oregon. So, defeated, and emotional eaters, we began to consume very small samples of the food. We drank a lot of the generic water.

The first full day out there we tore up the upholstery on our front seats. One seat provided us a bag in which to place both of our feet. I have an inherited foot condition that makes it quite painful to walk. That condition along with arthritis in my feet, and bad circulation kept my feet pretty cold. So, my life partner told me to take off my wet socks, and place my feet in the upholstered bag with his so that he could transfer heat from his feet to mine. I'll tell you, there is no brand name for that kind of love!

The other front seat upholstery was cut open and placed over our legs like a blanket. Atop of that was a liner bought to protect the car from our dog, Jake and all the hair he loses during his daily activities. These along with our jackets (Bear Ridge ™ and REI ™) made perfect layers and we only needed to run the engine full of gas from our local 76 ™ station in Tricity, Oregon every three or four hours. BTW, we did fill up before we left!

The first full day turned into the 2nd night, and probably another foot of snow fell. We could barely get our car door open to dispose of bodily fluids, or to scoop new snow cones for drinking. Egads! By now, we really, really knew we were in trouble.   I spied the ketchup placed in the middle console and realized that it had a pal from Kentucky Fried Chicken™ a small container of Honey Mustard. I asked my husband which he preferred and I shared with him the idea of a true gourmet dinner. Fine dining at its best. He refused my offer; I really don't know why. We ate plainer Kirkland ™ Lamb & Rice chow and drank lots and lots of generic (God freely given complete with dirt) water. That day I also looked at a friend's book that I needed to return, "Roberts Rules" copyright 1923, it looked like fire fodder to me. But, alas, I remembered again, we had no matches! I was sad indeed.
The 2nd full day came and we were up with the sunrise. Just like the day before we were having very deep and realistic conversations about if we were going to die. We were trying to figure out just how in the world, we could get someone's attention. As with the day before, every time we started the engine, we turned on our Duro ™ cell phone, and dialed 911, to no avail. At

the same time, we turned on our Vastfire ™ GPS, and pinged the minimum of four satellites each time.
I began to talk about how sad I would be if I died and my mother got the last word in our little tiff. My husband offered very kindly to walk to find a soul who might remedy our situation. He'd offered at least twice before. The problem was now; I didn't feel the need to disapprove of this very scary proposition. I was facing being alone possibly in the dark; you know a whole other night. I didn't like that! After all, the night has always been a very scary place to be for me!

or 10 minutes so that I could try and make it last at least a week. Being the emotional eater than I am, I was convinced that I was starving….and I put in my hand. Oh, glorious dog food, I tried not to puke I dipped it in honey mustard, and found out it was sad seconds to the ketchup. Just sayin'.

I had nothing more to do. My job it seemed was to survive so that I could live and see my man tomorrow. I didn't want any more of that Kirkland ™ lamb and rice! All wrapped up again, I looked outside; I saw a little bent over man. His bones were made of limbs of a tree, he wore a snow sombrero, snow cape, and snow pants. I was pretty sure by this time I was getting a little delirious- I got out the Bic ™ pen and paper wrote down the time, my activities, and the time since my man left. My little tree all wrapped up in snow clothes talked me to sleep and stayed with me for at least two hours. I turned on the engine at 2:30, I turned it off at 2:55. At 3:00 I noted it had been about 6 hours, I prayed that I'd see or hear

Someone, anyone, in less than an hour.

At 3:15 – I noted two crosses on the window, God holding us in his arms, leaving us in his Grace, sending his message that we were indeed safe. I looked again, and there the crosses still stood, a husband and wife, arms intertwined facing the world. Thank you,

God, for sending the message. I am still alive and I will live… I just need patience…

I wanted to stay in this world.

I settled back down, and I wrapped myself up. I told myself that soon, I was sure I'd see a real person. Soon my eyes were closed, there was really nothing else to do…. I felt the cold air hit my pretty warm face.

I told myself… that I was worth the fight.

I honored myself a beautiful woman, loved with delight.

I remembered that #shepersisted—and I knew that I, too, was at least that good.

The thoughts swirled and swirled inside my head, and when I heard that beautiful young man….

"Clyde… Is that you...??" "Clyde….am I mad??"

"No ma'am, I'm Ryan, I work for the United States Forest Department"

Oh MY GOD! I'd just seen my first ANGEL!!

This angel, **handsome** was he, he checked my fuel and assured me I could run my engine freely. Instructions were to keep warm and wait, he had sent off for help, I only needed patience for perhaps, 2 hours. Best of all he'd seen my wonderful husband and HE WAS OKAY.

The very first tears fell… happy was I. But it didn't take long for me to mop up my mess, I still had at least 2 hours to wait. I checked the time at least every 15 minutes it seemed, I looked at the Kirkland™ Lamb & Rice and promised not to eat it! And I was pretty much done with that dirty damned bucket!

Pretty much two hours later, along came two more very handsome angels named Ken and Kehoe, Jr. I have to admit my eyes were on fire, I met so many young, handsome angels—I simply could not believe my luck, surely, I was in HEAVAN. I will never forget how hard they worked to force the little vehicle down the path. At the bottom was Ryan's Forest Ranger partner to drive me on by, to an ambulance for checking vitals. The men there too, delighted mine visions—Tiller paramedics will never be forgotten. We passed so many people; I could not believe what I saw. Trucks and trucks from the Douglas County Sherriff, and Search and Rescue, too. We stopped a couple of times so my chariot driver to speak to a few, the men outside were full of smiles—I was really happy too. My driver offered me nibbles of carrots, peppers, and broccoli, but I thought it was his lunch, and he looked so perfect and healthy, surely, he worked hard, and needed nourishment…I could not take his lunch. How did all these parents do it, raise so many perfectly shaped men?! Oh, I could barely take it, they were all very sweet, considerate young men. Might I say here and now, that I take it all back, there are out there, somewhere, quite a few REALLY GOOD MEN.

Next stop we met Kehoe, Sr. and a nice lady with a cookie and coffee. I don't like coffee and yet it turned out that it was manna from heaven!! I was dropped off at the ambulance, my husband was there, my blood sugars were perfect, I remembered the name of YOUR F****** PRESIDENT! My heart rate was a little fast, we discussed our options, and I said I want to go home and take my medicine.

Jerry came by and we got in to his truck. He took us both homes, back to Tricity…to my babies, my heaven. We showered; we shaved, brushed our teeth—called his mother. Called my sister. Posted to Facebook—one little message. Laid down in the most comfortable bed on earth, held my man, thanked him profusely, and said thank heavens.

I'm warm, I am dry, I'm fed, and I'm happy. I know who I am, what I need, what I can share, what I love… My kids, my husband, my family, my friends, those beautiful angels who showed up by the dozens… I am thankful to all, and offer to share my bear hugs from Jesus…
I was released March 10, 2017—from a hell created by myself and reborn new, beautiful, and sweet.

I hope you never have to live through such days, but if you do…. just focus on what is really important to you. I promise you'll make it and come out more beautiful too!!!

Dear Costco—what do you think?? My poor dog is missing some food from his bowl! Do you send out coupons that Jake might appreciate? I hope you don't mind indulging his master's silly old wife!!

Sincerely, Peggy A. Rowe-Snyder

Note: All copyrighted and trademarked material used in this humorous letter belong to their various companies and title holders. The names are used because their products were actually in the car. This is not an endorsement nor a discouragement of the use of any product named. This letter was constructed for the express purpose of creating laughter, and calming nerves.

The Cost of being "Famous"

Posted on March 17, 2017

One last thought for today. Kind of interesting, I guess..... Our street goes into a cross street and they make a "T" where they come together. We were turning onto our street, bringing the car home. The guy who was on our street, watched us turn on, and then made a U turn in the "T" and followed us and went by really slow past our drive way. He went up the road, turned around and went by again, looking.... on the phone... I can just imagine it...."Dude, I found where those people stuck on the mountain lives...." Geez! And I think this why? I walked into a store yesterday in south Roseburg. (Southgate) Cashier looks at me.... and then loudly (and remember I'm 1/2 deaf, so if I say it's loud).... "How'd you like it up there on that mountain top? Bet you were scared shitless!! God sure had his hand on you didn't he?" He never waited for an answer... he ASSUMED he knew.... Bet, I wasn't scared shitless!!! Not most the time anyhow. LOL

Note: All the attention we got during our short time of being 'famous' folks were very kind and supportive. Most said they'd prayed for us. Others let us know they were happy we survived. Some kept track of the progress (think law enforcement wife). Even Peg's hair dresser recognized her and had questions and positive words.

IF You Have Read This Far...

You are a glutton for punishment. But I thank you for your support from the bottom of my heart on behalf of myself and my family. Your support through this book, I hope, will buy a sick man another Jeep and/or make it so that I can support myself if needed. I want to stay in Tricity. Some of it will pay tuition at Oregon State (Yup, I'm a Beaver Girl now). I have promised myself to not waste my time here on Earth. I will continue on my mission in life, trying to heal those who need it, trying to help people and animals. And by spreading The Good News of the power of God and his/her/its wonderous works.

Thank you so much, Peggy

All photos in this publication were taken March 5th, 2017, the day we went 'missing', 'lost', 'stuck'. All were taken along the South Umpqua River at one place or another. All were taken by Peggy A. Rowe-Snyder and are wholly original and owned by herself. In this set is an image of Clyde (her husband) taking a photo on that day.

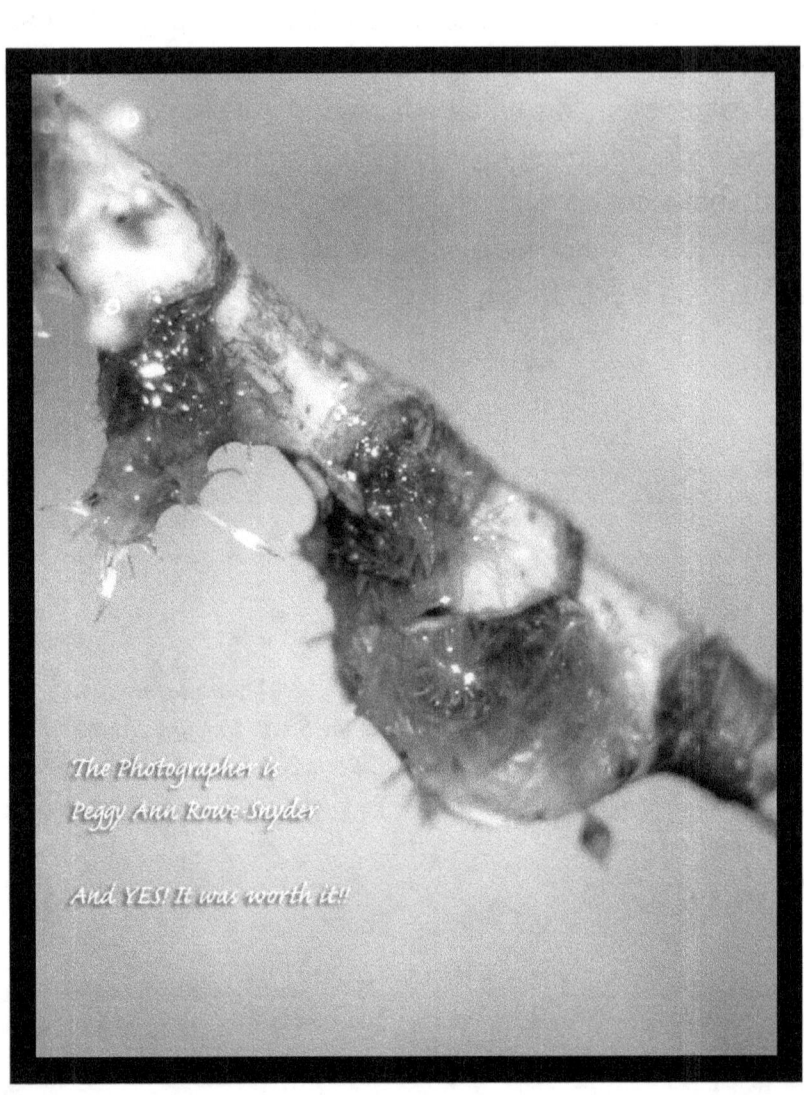

The Photographer is
Peggy Ann Rowe-Snyder

And YES! It was worth it!!

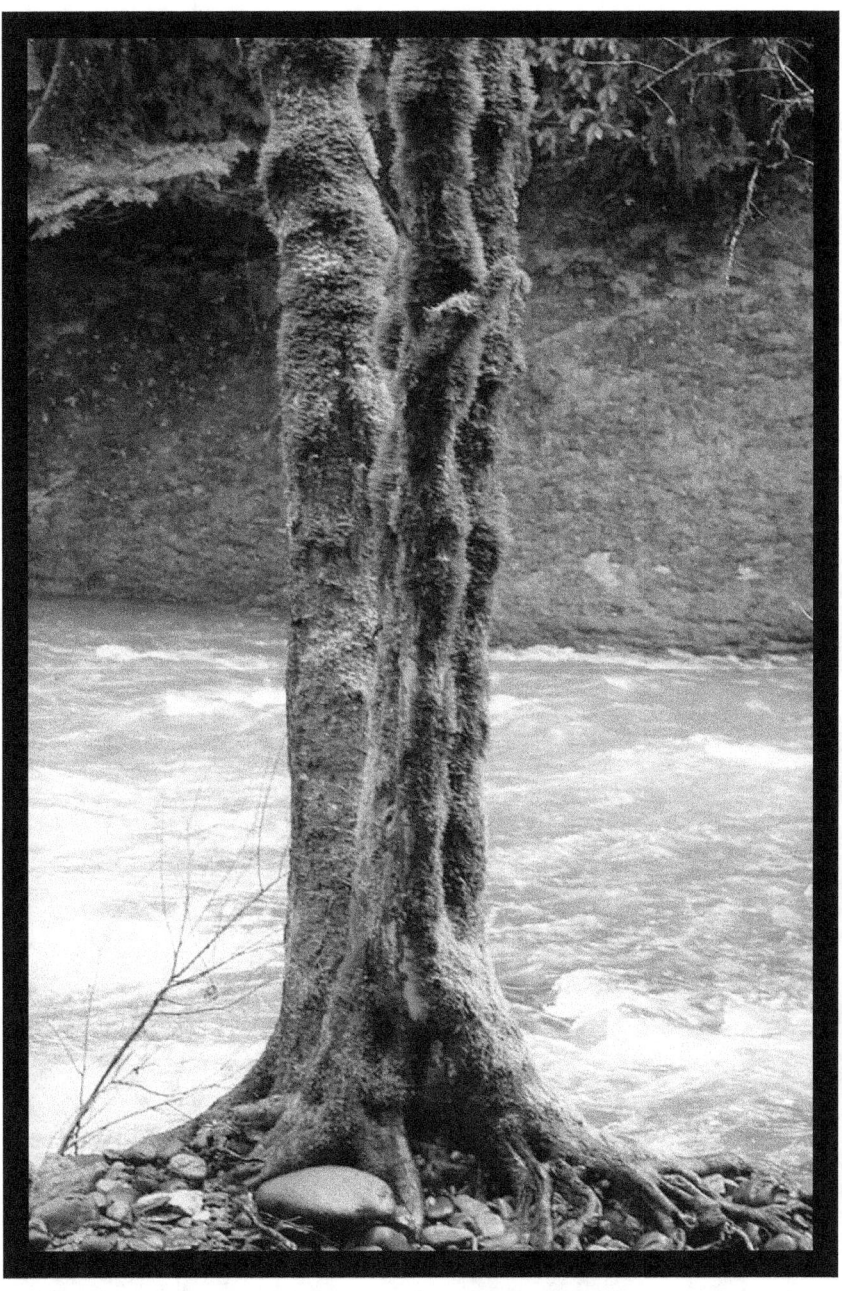

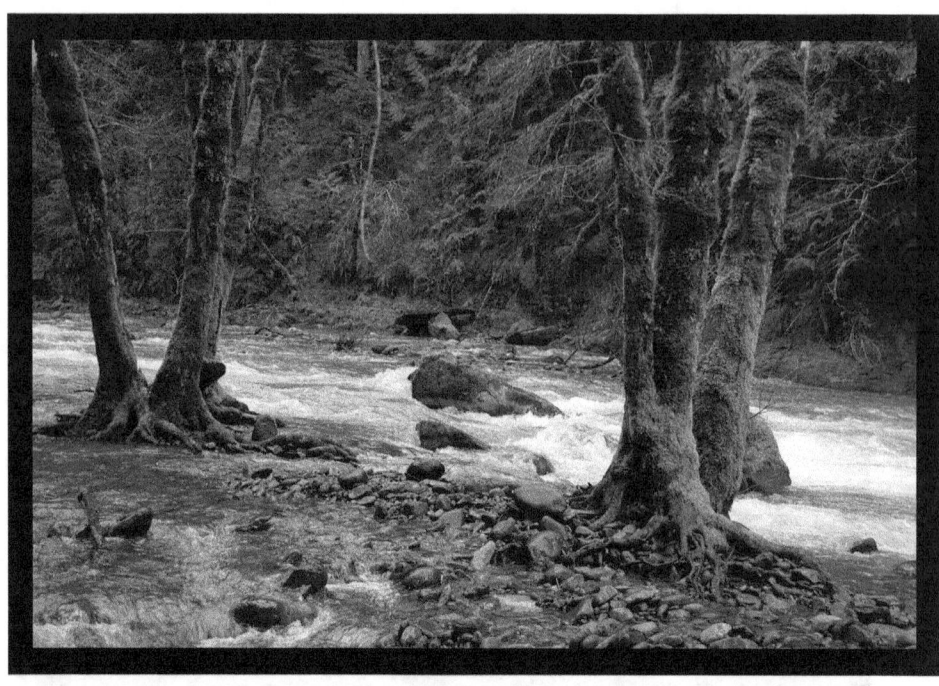

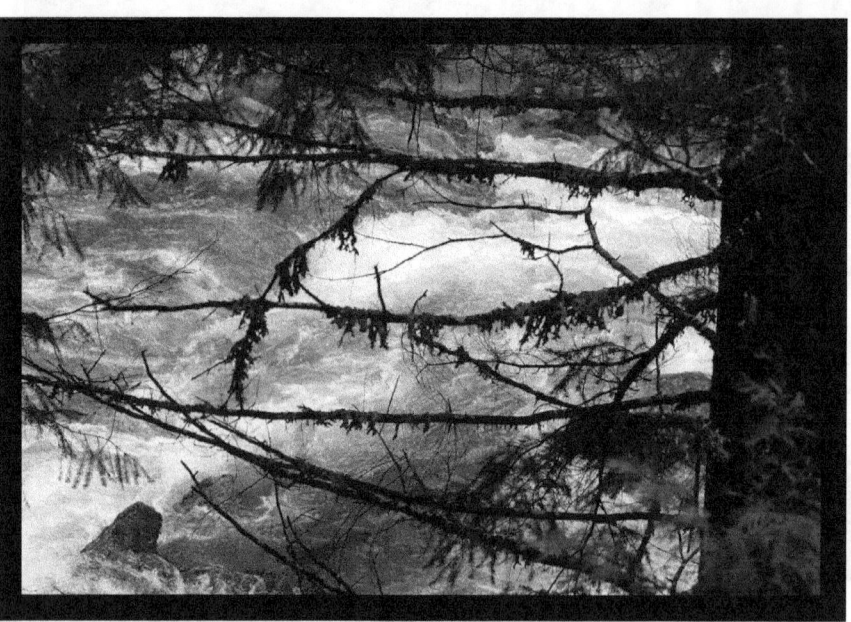

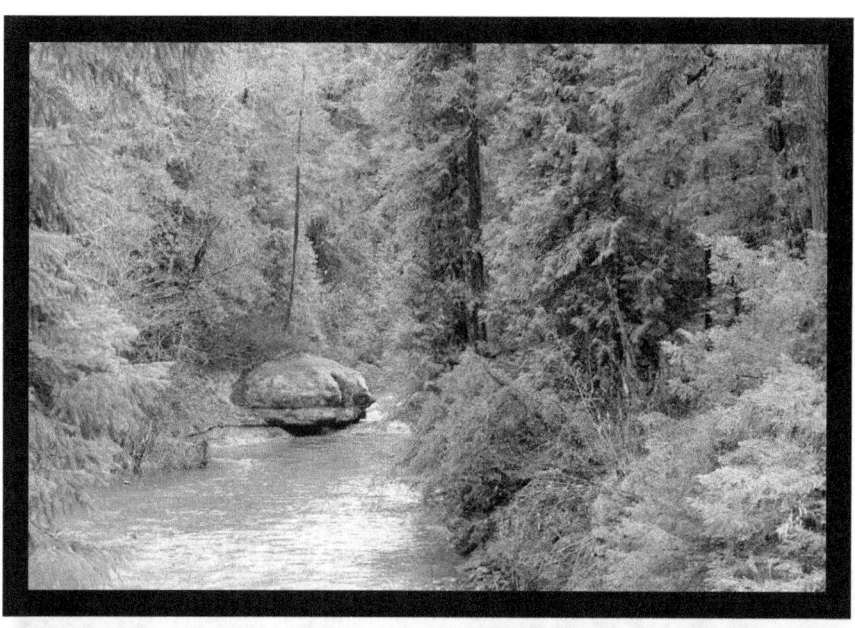

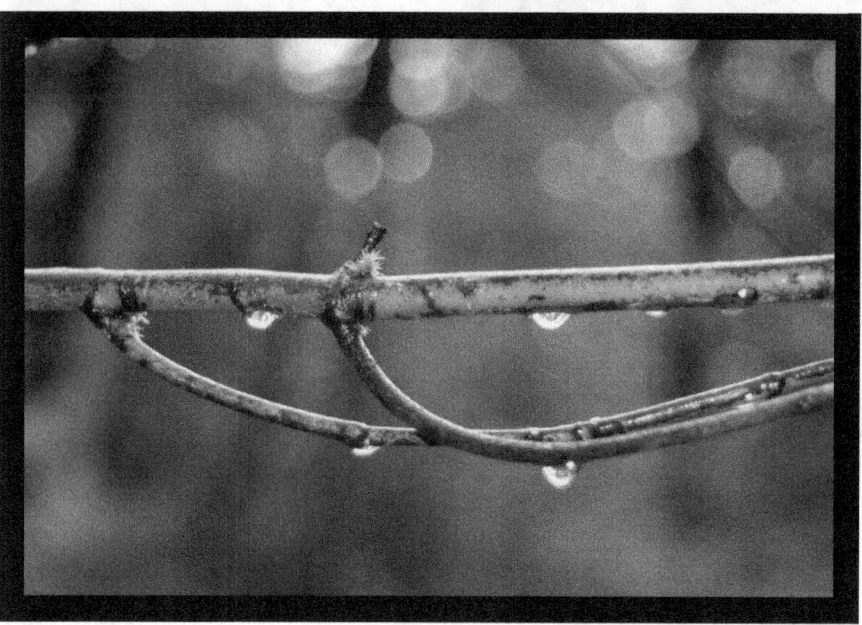

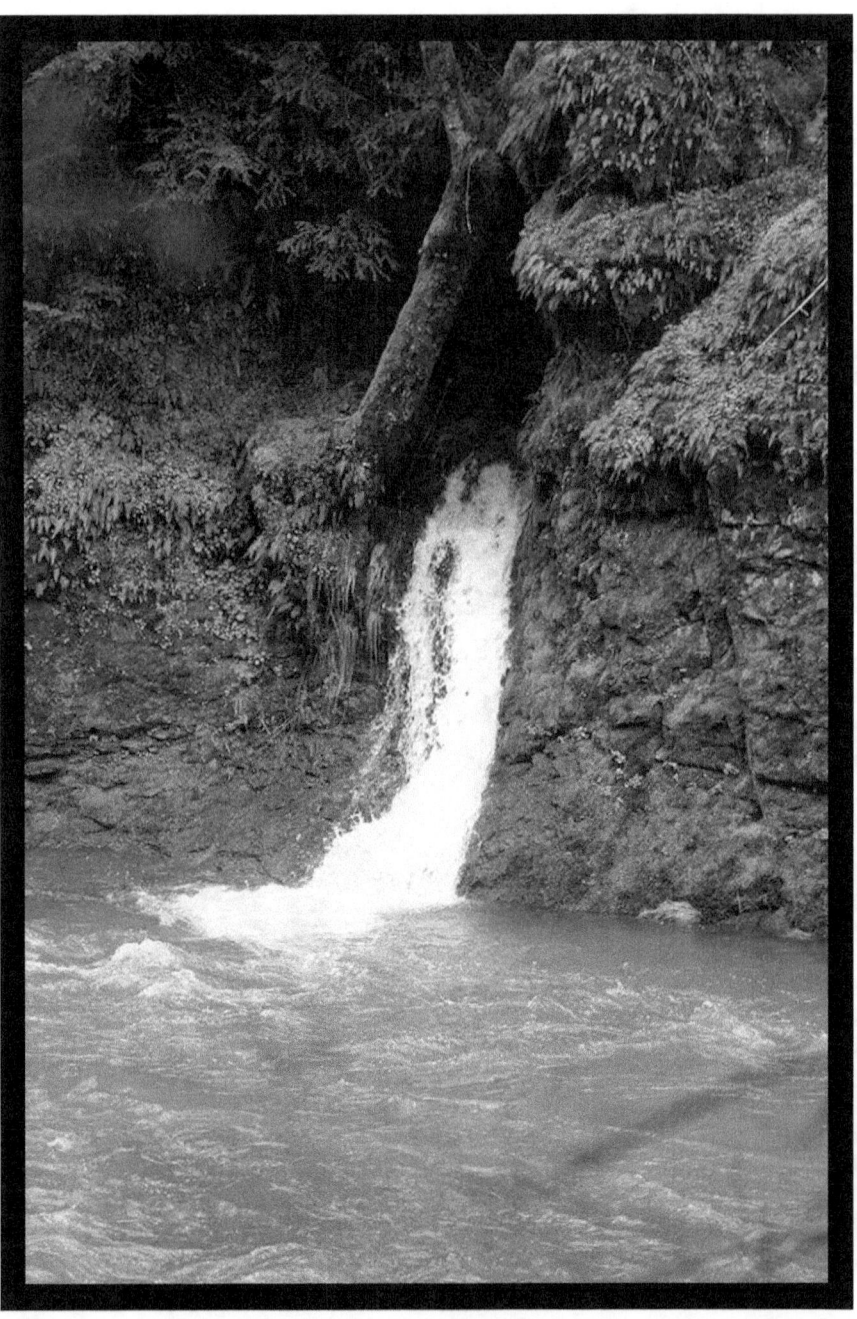

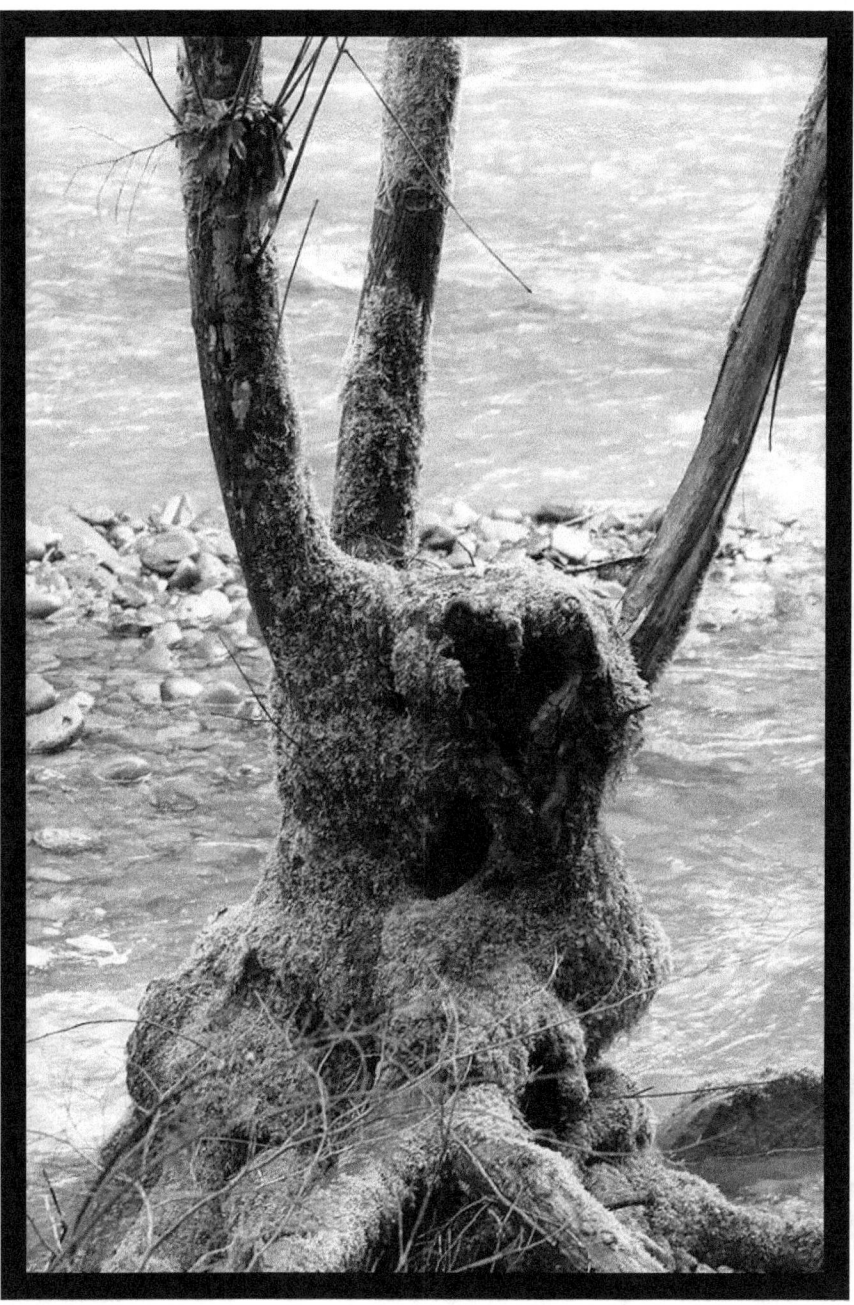

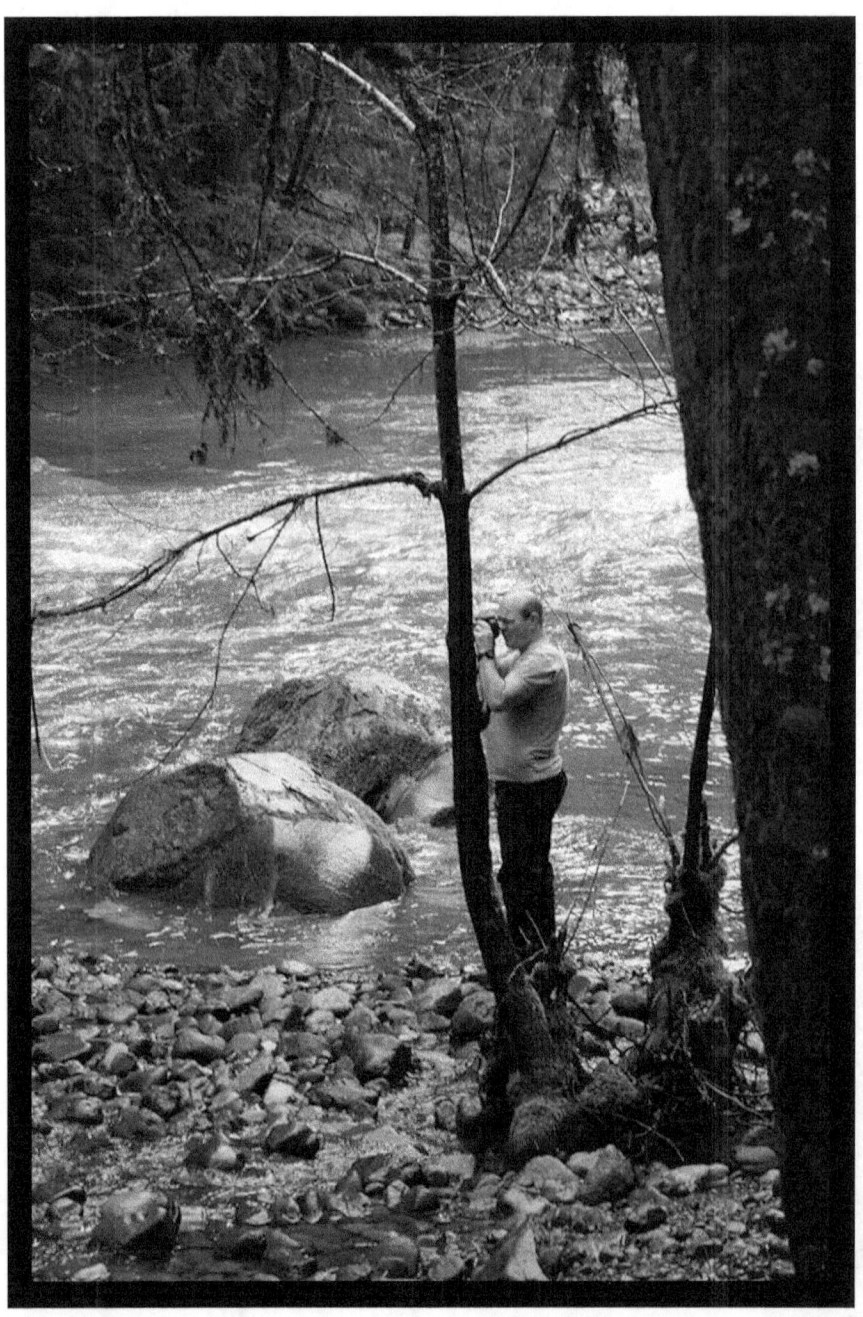

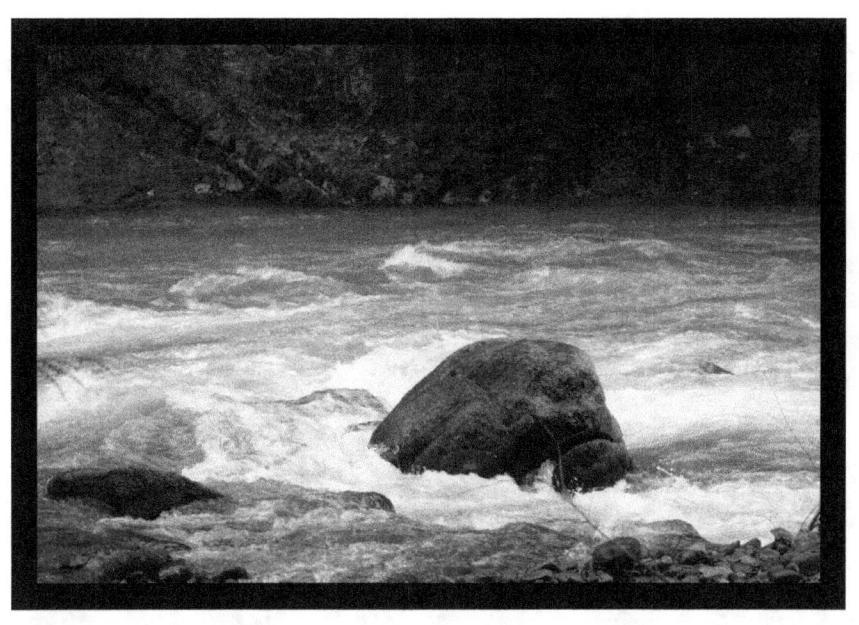

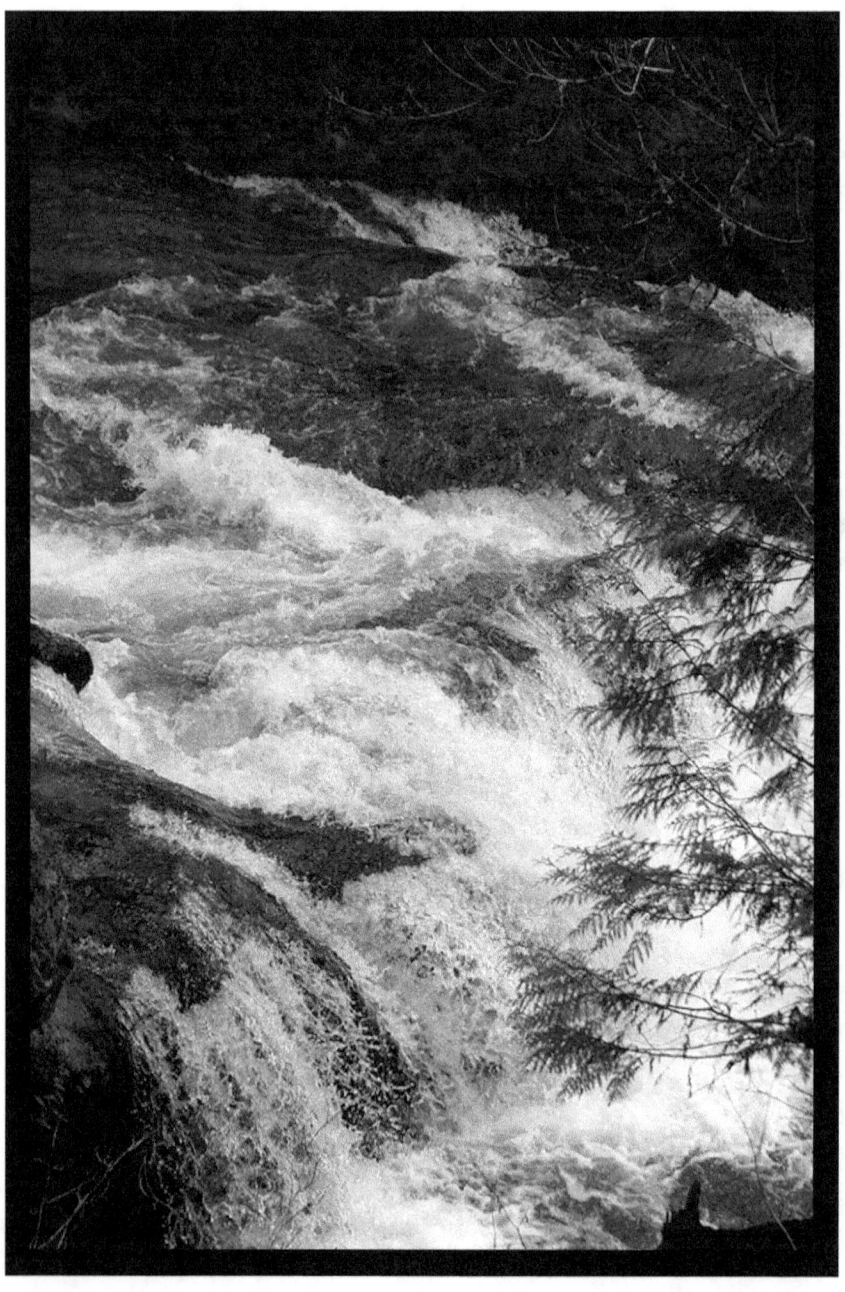

Sources:

Most of this story comes out of my memory. As it was, we who lived this story. I also picked my husband's brain to be sure I remembered right. To guide my memory, I also used these websites and books:

Google Maps
From Canyonville to Tiller is approximately 23 miles.
Tiller to Ash Flat Campground is 18 miles.
South Umpqua Falls is literally only a few miles from Ash Flat Campground, after crossing Coyote Creek.

https://www.cowcreek.com/tribal-story/

My profile at www.facebook.com
My Blog: www.pegrowe.com

About the Author: *Peggy A Rowe-Snyder*

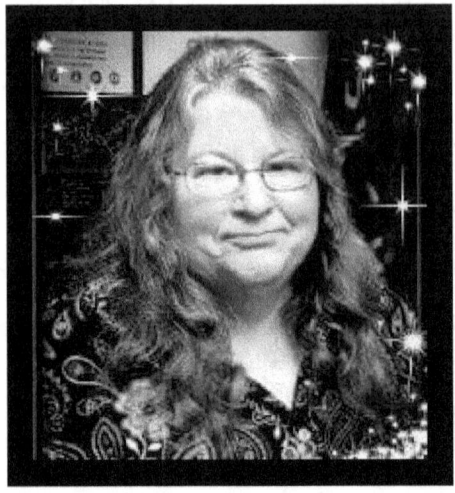

Born in the San Francisco Bay Area East Bay in 1962. Raised in Newark, California in Alameda County. Spent ten years in Sonoma County where she attended Santa Rosa Junior College and earned her AS/and Small PC Technician Certificate. During this time, she honed her Historical Society skills with the Cloverdale Historical Society where she sat on the board. She ran her own computer consultant company and worked other jobs to support her young family as a single mother. Computer Consultant, Website Designer, Goddess of Geek, Former President of Douglas County Historical Society, Editor, author, & lay-out artist of the Umpqua Trapper for about 10 years. Mother of Four, Student at Oregon State University. Survivor of childhood sexual abuse and domestic violence during her first marriage. She still lives in Tricity on a place that sits atop a section of the old Applegate Trail. She dreams about starting an Airbnb since she lives only four miles from 7 Feathers Casino. The business will include the ability to house people's pets. She hopes this business will pay for the house and someone to care for a ½ acre of landscaping.

She believes in self responsibility, self-integrity, and self-care. Honesty, compassion and empathy are her rule of law. Protecting women and children from any type of abuse is her lifelong ambition. She hopes to obtain a BS at Oregon State University with a major in History and a minor in Women's Studies and use that knowledge to further two loves – History and Women.

www.ingramcontent.com/pod-product-compliance
Lightning Source LLC
Chambersburg PA
CBHW072206170526
45158CB00004BB/1785